The Owl in the Tower

By Cameron Macintosh

Mim's town had a very high clock tower.

The tower was home to a big owl.

But the clock tower was not safe.

"That tower could crash down,"
Dad said.
"I will help make a new tower."

"What about the owl?" said Mim.
"It has a nest in the tower!"

"Don't frown, Mim," said Dad.
"We can find it a new home."

Mim spotted a high tree.

Let's make a house for the owl in that tree.

"I will make the house out of wood," said Dad.

He made a little house with a big hole in it.

Then Dad sat the wood house high up in the tree.

"Wow, that is a great house for the owl!" said Mim.

But the owl did not go into the house.

The owl went out to hunt.

It got a mouse in its mouth.

It went back into the tower.

"How can we get that owl
to go in the house?" said Mim.

"Let's make a soft nest," said Dad.

Mim got sticks and leaves.

Dad put them up in the house.

The next day, the owl was looking out of the house!